W9-BFM-054

SILVER BURDETT *Centennial* SONGBOOK

SILVER BURDETT COMPANY   MORRISTOWN, NJ

Atlanta, GA • Cincinnati, OH • Dallas, TX • Northfield, IL • San Carlos, CA • Agincourt, Ontario

A Greeting from the President of Silver Burdett

Dear Educator:

Since 1885, Silver Burdett Company has published music textbooks for schools. Throughout these one hundred years, the Company has kept in close touch with teachers, responding to their opinions and their professional needs.

In the late 1880s, Edgar O. Silver, founder of the Company, made a survey of "the condition of music education in the United States." Since that time, thousands of teachers have shared their opinions and their expertise with Silver Burdett. This information has been of great importance in shaping the content of our publications during the first century of the Company's existence.

In 1983, we sent out a survey asking educators to list for us their favorite songs--the songs that have been the most useful in their classrooms. We received responses from more than 17,000 music teachers, classroom teachers, supervisors, and principals.

The Silver Burdett Centennial Songbook has been compiled from that survey. It contains the songs that led the list in number of votes, and they are placed in the book in the order of their popularity. Most of the first fifty songs have appeared in Silver Burdett's music textbooks at some time in our history. For the centennial songbook, many of the songs have been reproduced from our music publications, old and new.

We thank all who participated in the survey, and we hope all music educators will enjoy using the Silver Burdett Centennial Songbook. We offer this book to you with the sincere wish that the partnership between educators and Silver Burdett Company will continue for a second century.

Sincerely,

Patrick Donaghy
President

Patrick Donaghy, President of Silver Burdett, signs the letter on this page. He is seated at the desk used by Edgar O. Silver in the first office of Silver Burdett in 1885. The desk is now in the lobby of the company's headquarters in Morristown, New Jersey.

Contents

The songs are sequenced in the order determined by the responses to the centennial songbook survey. The song with the most nominations is first in order. Two songs that ranked in the top fifty are not included in the Silver Burdett Centennial Songbook because problems involving the right to reprint them could not be resolved. They are "God Bless America," which would have followed "Marching to Pretoria," and "Rudolph the Red-Nosed Reindeer," which would have followed "Billy Boy."

Workshops
Where Teacher and Publisher Meet

In the summer of 1884, Hosea E. Holt, a supervisor of music in the Boston public schools, organized a summer school for music supervisors. Holt was coauthor, with John W. Tufts, of a new series of textbooks called THE NORMAL MUSIC COURSE.

Edgar O. Silver, a young employee in a publishing house, visited Holt's summer music class. He was impressed with Holt's teaching method, and with THE NORMAL MUSIC COURSE. Less than a year later, in April 1885, Edgar Silver purchased the rights to THE NORMAL MUSIC COURSE and founded Silver Burdett Company.

Edgar Silver had worked in the textbook business for two years. He had seen textbooks handled simply as products, sometimes

Hosea Holt's 1884 summer music school gave impetus to the founding of Silver Burdett Company. Mr. Holt is shown seated at the far left; Edgar Silver, founder of the company, is seated on the grass, at the right front.

sold in the general store, along with groceries, dry goods and farm supplies. He believed that a textbook publisher should know about the real needs of teachers, and should create textbooks that would meet those needs. A summer school seemed the ideal place for teachers and publisher to get together.

In the summer of 1885, soon after founding Silver Burdett, Edgar Silver cosponsored the second session of Hosea Holt's summer school. The school became an annual event, a tradition that has continued from that day to this. In 1983 there were five Silver Burdett music workshops in the United States, all offering college credit. The interchange of ideas between teacher and publisher, which led to the formation of the company, still enriches the textbooks that come from Silver Burdett today.

In 1983, one hundred sixteen teachers and supervisors attended the Silver Burdett workshop at Appalachian State University at Boone, North Carolina. Other 1983 workshops were held at the University of Utah, Salt Lake City; Bridgewater State College, Bridgewater, Massachusetts; California State University, Los Angeles; Xavier University, Cincinnati, Ohio; and Fontbonne College, St. Louis, Missouri.

Music Textbooks from *Silver Burdett*

1885

THE NORMAL MUSIC COURSE

Hosea Holt and John W. Tufts

"One is not musically skilled until he thoroughly knows how the notes will sound as he mentally reads them, or knows the exact representation when he simply hears them."

–*Third Reader, p. 4*

1900

THE MODERN MUSIC SERIES

Robert Foresman and Eleanor Smith

". . . while presenting the most beautiful and interesting exercises and songs selected from the great song writers, (this series) furnishes at the same time a most complete, consistent and logical plan of developing the power to read music in a purely musical way."

–*Second Book, p. 4*

1914

THE PROGRESSIVE MUSIC SERIES

Horatio Parker, Osbourne McConathy, Edward Bailey Birge, Otto W. Miessner

". . . the teaching of singing, of artistic interpretation with beautiful tone quality, should be the constant aim in public-school music."

–*Teacher's Manual for First, Second and Third Grades*

The First Hundred Years

1927

THE MUSIC HOUR

Osbourne McConathy, W. Otto Miessner, Edward Bailey Birge and Mabel E. Bray

". . . music shall make the child happier and more sensitive to beauty and, as a socializing force, shall enable him to adjust . . . to his environment"

–Elementary Teacher's Book

1944

NEW MUSIC HORIZONS

Osbourne McConathy, Russell V. Morgan, James L. Mursell, Marshall Bartholomew, Mabel E. Bray, W. Otto Miessner, Edward Bailey Birge

Music teachers should "stress the personal, social, and aesthetic values of the art of music as a source of enjoyment and an avenue of self-expression."

–Accompaniments and Interpretation for the Teacher

1956

MUSIC FOR LIVING

James L. Mursell, Gladys Tipton, Beatrice Landeck, Harriet Nordholm, Roy E. Freeburg, Jack M. Watson

Music offers children
–pleasure
–emotional release and satisfaction
–creative self-expression
–self-fulfillment through experiences of success
–the discipline of achievement
–manifold experiences of sharing and cooperating with others
–enrichment for all the years to come

–Teacher's Editions

1964

MAKING MUSIC YOUR OWN

Elizabeth Crook (1–6), Lawrence Eisman (7–8), Mary Jaye (K), Elizabeth Jones (7–8), Beatrice Landeck (1–6), Raymond Malone (7–8), Harold Youngberg (1–6)

"Through participation in a variety of musical activities and acquaintance with a unique selection of song and listening materials, [the child] gains music skills and forms music concepts, becoming aware of both the expressiveness and the discipline of the musical art."

–Teacher's Editions

1974–1985

SILVER BURDETT MUSIC

Neva Aubin (K), Elizabeth Crook (K–6), Erma Hayden (K), Mary E. Hoffman (7–8), Albert McNeil (7–8), Bennett Reimer (1–8), David S. Walker (K–6)

"A child conceptualizes about music when he describes a fundamental idea about (1) the inner working of music (melody, rhythm, harmony, form, tone color), (2) the roles of music in human life, (3) styles of music, or (4) the relationship of music to the other arts."

–Teacher's Editions

Love Letters to Silver Burdett

music series – keep up the good work!

Thank you for a good
C. B., Spencer, Wis.

In a sea of mediocrity, you have not lowered your standards. Your materials have brought both learning and great pleasure to the children and to me.

J. K., San Francisco, Calif.

my privilege to use Silver Burdett books for forty years! It has been
L. C. N., Richardson, Tex.

SILVER BURDETT !
I LOVE YOU !

B. T., New York, N.Y.

am really enjoying the current edition of Silver Burdett.
D. R. H., Farmington, N.M.

Silver Burdeth is certainly an old friend ..... B. C., Lothian, Md.

I have a deep appreciation for your listening program, It is the best program that I have ever seen ..... R. S. B., Lafayette, La.

We enjoy your books.
Congratulations on your birthday
E. M., Nanuet, N.Y.

I would like to take this opportunity to tell you how much I have enjoyed using Silver Burdett materials.
R. N., Hinsdale, N.H.

Silver-B !
We love you.
P. H., Detroit, Mich.

You do consistently good work - Thanks !!
B. L., Cheyenne, Wy.

This Land Is Your Land

Words and Music by Woody Guthrie

Arranged by Bruce Simpson

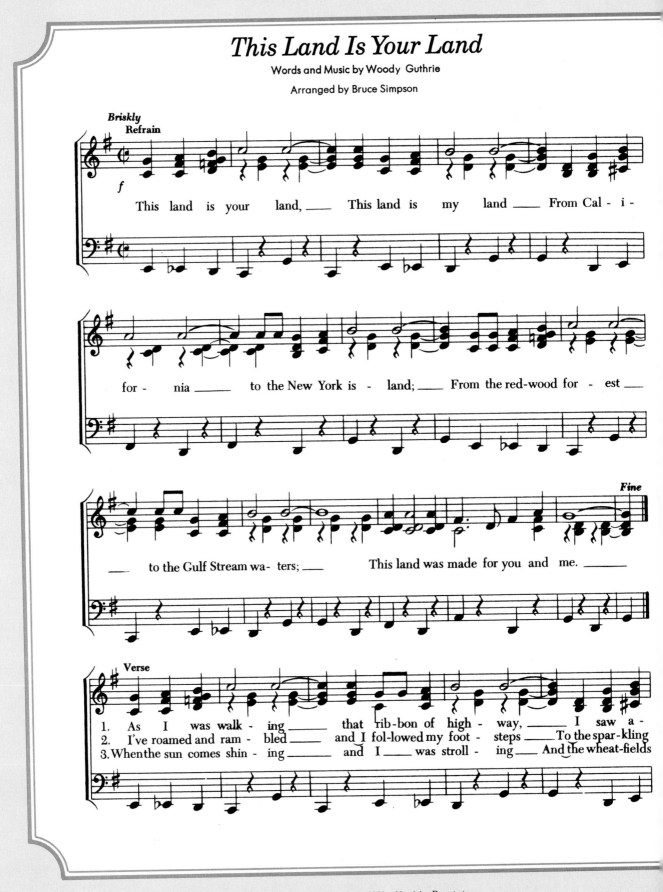

This land is your land, ___ This land is my land ___ From Cal - i -

for - nia ___ to the New York is - land; ___ From the red-wood for - est

___ to the Gulf Stream wa- ters; ___ This land was made for you and me. ___

1. As I was walk - ing ___ that rib-bon of high - way, ___ I saw a -
2. I've roamed and ram - bled ___ and I fol-lowed my foot - steps ___ To the spar-kling
3. When the sun comes shin - ing ___ and I ___ was stroll - ing ___ And the wheat-fields

bove me _____ that end-less sky - way. _____ I saw be - low me _____
sands of _____ her dia -mond des - erts, _____ And all a - round me _____
wav - ing _____ and the dust clouds roll - ing, _____ As the fog was lift - ing _____

D.C. al Fine

_ that gold-en val - ley, _____ This land was made for you and me. _____
_ a voice was sound-ing,_____ "This land was made for you and me."_____
_ a voice was chant - ing, _____ "This land was made for you and me." _____

8va

In 1895, Silver Burdett Company published a book called *Poems of Home and Country* by Rev. Samuel Francis Smith, D.D. One of the poems in the book was "America" (My Country! Tis of thee), which Smith had written in 1832. This old photograph shows Smith at Edgar O. Silver's desk in the company's headquarters. On page ii, Patrick Donaghy, who is now president of Silver Burdett, is shown seated at this desk.

MY COUNTRY! 'TIS OF THEE.

1. My coun - try! 'tis of thee, Sweet land of lib - er - ty, Of thee I
2. My na - tive coun - try, thee— Land of the no - ble free— Thy name—I
3. Let mu - sic swell the breeze, And ring from all the trees Sweet freedom's
4. Our fa-thers' God! to Thee, Au - thor of lib - er - ty, To Thee we

sing; Land where my fa - thers died! Land of the pil - grims' pride!
love; I love thy rocks and rills, Thy woods and tem - pled hills:
song: Let mor - tal tongues a - wake; Let all that breathe par - take;
sing; Long may our Land be bright With free - dom's ho - ly light,

From ev - ery moun - tain side Let free - dom ring!
My heart with rap - ture thrills, Like that a - bove.
Let rocks their si - lence break,—The sound pro - long.
Pro - tect us by Thy might, Great God, our King!

S. F. SMITH

Bingo

AMERICAN FOLK SONG

ARRANGED BY FRANCIS GIRARD

Happily

There was a farm-er had a dog, And Bin-go was his name - o.

B - I - N - G - O, B - I - N - G - O,

B - I - N - G - O, And Bin-go was his name - o.

America, the Beautiful

KATHARINE LEE BATES

SAMUEL A. WARD

Majestically

1. O beau - ti-ful for spacious skies, For amber waves of grain, ___ For pur - ple moun-tain
2. O beau-ti-ful for pil-grim feet Whose stern impassion'd stress ___ A thor-ough-fare for
3. O beau - ti - ful for he-roes prov'd In lib-er-at-ing strife, ___ Who more than self their
4. O beau - ti - ful for pa-triot dream That sees beyond the years Thine al - a - bas - ter

maj - es-ties A - bove the fruit-ed plain. ___ A - mer - i - ca! A - mer - i - ca! God
free-dom beat A - cross the wil-der - ness. ___ A - mer - i - ca! A - mer - i - ca! God
coun-try lov'd And mer-cy more than life. ___ A - mer - i - ca! A - mer - i - ca! May
cit - ies gleam, Undimm'd by hu-man tears. ___ A - mer - i - ca! A - mer - i - ca! God

shed His grace on thee, ___ And crown thy good with brotherhood From sea to shin-ing sea.
mend thine ev-'ry flaw, ___ Con - firm thy soul in self-con-trol, Thy lib - er - ty in law.
God thy gold re - fine ___ Till all suc-cess be no - ble-ness, And ev'ry gain di - vine.
shed His grace on thee, ___ And crown thy good with brotherhood From sea to shin-ing sea.

Music from The Music Hour, Lower Grades   Copyright Silver Burdett Company 1934   Art from Music in Our Life   © Silver Burdett Company 1959

Yankee Doodle

WORDS AND MUSIC TRADITIONAL

Yan- kee Doo- dle came to town, Rid- ing on a po - ny;

Stuck a feath- er in his cap And called it Mac - a - ro - ni.

Yan- kee Doo -dle keep it up, Yan- kee Doo- dle dan - dy,

Mind the mu- sic and the step And with the girls be hand- y.

 Music and art from Music for Living, Book 2 © Silver Burdett Company 1956

It's a Small World

ARRANGED BY DAVID FIORENZA

The Star-Spangled Banner

Francis Scott Key   John Stafford Smith

1. Oh, __ say! can you see, by the dawn's ear - ly light, What so proud - ly we
2. On the shore, dim - ly seen through the mists of the deep, Where the foe's haugh - ty
3. Oh, __ thus be it ever when __ free men shall stand Be - tween their loved

hailed at the twi - light's last gleam - ing, Whose broad stripes and bright stars, through the
host in dread si - lence re - pos - es, What is that which the breeze, o'er the
homes and the war's des - o - la - tion! Blest with vic - t'ry and peace, may the

THIS OLD MAN

English Singing Game

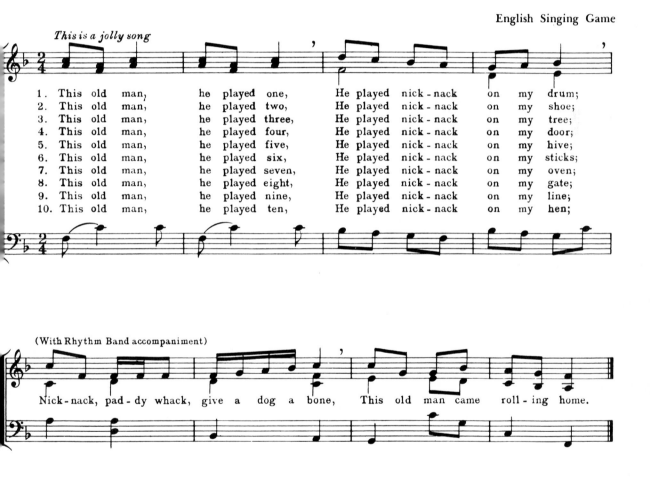

This is a jolly song

1. This old man, he played one, He played nick-nack on my drum;
2. This old man, he played two, He played nick-nack on my shoe;
3. This old man, he played three, He played nick-nack on my tree;
4. This old man, he played four, He played nick-nack on my door;
5. This old man, he played five, He played nick-nack on my hive;
6. This old man, he played six, He played nick-nack on my sticks;
7. This old man, he played seven, He played nick-nack on my oven;
8. This old man, he played eight, He played nick-nack on my gate;
9. This old man, he played nine, He played nick-nack on my line;
10. This old man, he played ten, He played nick-nack on my hen;

(With Rhythm Band accompaniment)

Nick-nack, pad-dy whack, give a dog a bone, This old man came roll-ing home.

Music and art from New Music Horizons, Second Book   *Copyright by Silver Burdett Company 1944*

Don Gato

English Words by Margaret Marks   Mexican Folk Song
Arranged by Alice Firgau

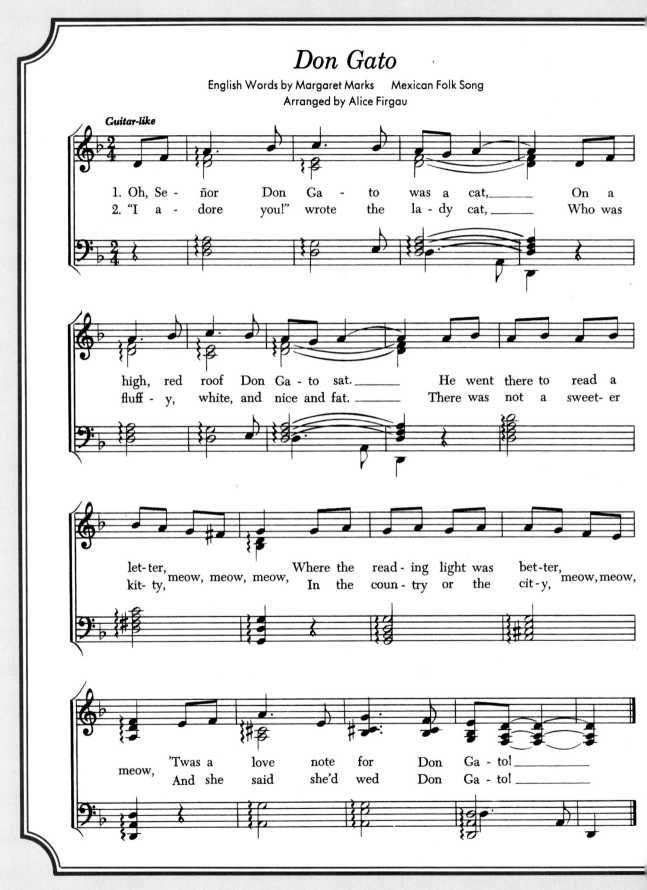

1. Oh, Se - ñor Don Ga - to was a cat,_____ On a
2. "I a - dore you!" wrote the la - dy cat,_____ Who was

high, red roof Don Ga - to sat._____ He went there to read a
fluff - y, white, and nice and fat. _____ There was not a sweet- er

let - ter, meow, meow, meow, Where the read - ing light was bet - ter, meow, meow,
kit - ty, In the coun - try or the cit - y,

meow, 'Twas a love note for Don Ga - to!_____
And she said she'd wed Don Ga - to!_____

3. Oh, Don Gato jumped so happily
   He fell off the roof and broke his knee,
   Broke his ribs and all his whiskers, meow, meow, meow,
   And his little solar plexus, meow, meow, meow,
   "¡Ay, caramba!" cried Don Gato!

4. Then the doctors all came on the run
   Just to see if something could be done,
   And they held a consultation, meow, meow, meow,
   About how to save their patient, meow, meow, meow,
   How to save Señor Don Gato!

5. But in spite of everything they tried
   Poor Señor Don Gato up and died,
   Oh, it wasn't very merry, meow, meow, meow,
   Going to the cemetery, meow, meow, meow,
   For the ending of Don Gato!

6. When the funeral passed the market square
   Such a smell of fish was in the air
   Though his burial was slated, meow, meow, meow,
   He became re-animated! meow, meow, meow,
   He came back to life, Don Gato!

15

Battle Hymn of the Republic

Julia Ward Howe   William Steffe

Descant by Evelyn H. Hunt

1. Mine eyes have seen the glo - ry of the com - ing of the Lord; He is
2. He has sound - ed forth the trum - pet that shall nev - er call re - treat; He is

tramp - ling out the vin - tage where the grapes of wrath are stored; He hath
sift - ing out the hearts of men be - fore the judg - ment seat. Oh, be

loosed the fate - ful light - ning of His ter - ri - ble swift sword; His truth is march - ing on.
swift, my soul, to an - swer Him! Be ju - bi - lant, my feet! Our God is march - ing on.

Music from Making Music Your Own, Book 5 © *Silver Burdett Company 1965* *Art from New Music Horizons, Fourth Book Copyright by Silver Burdett Company 1945*

17

Erie Canal

TRADITIONAL   OLD AMERICAN FOLK SONG

I got a mule, her name is Sal, Fif-teen miles on the
Git up there, Sal, we passed that lock, Fif-teen miles on the

E - rie Ca - nal!__ She's a good old work-er and a good old pal,
E - rie Ca - nal!__ And __ we'll make Rome _'fore__ six o' - clock,

Fif-teen miles on the E - rie Ca - nal!__ We've hauled some barg - es
Fif-teen miles on the E - rie Ca - nal!__ Just one more trip and

in our day, Filled with lum - ber, coal and hay, And
back we'll go Through the rain and sleet and snow, 'Cause

d min   g min   A₇   d min

we know ev - 'ry inch of the way From Al - ba-ny___ to ___
we know ev - 'ry inch of the way From Al - ba-ny___ to ___

A₇ d min C₇ REFRAIN   C₇

Buf - fa - lo.___ Low bridge, ev - 'ry-bod - y down,
Buf - fa - lo.___

F   C₇   F

Low bridge, 'cause we're com - ing to a town, And you'll

C₇   F   C₇

al - ways know your neigh-bor; You'll al-ways know your pal, If you

F   B♭   F C₇   F

ev - er nav - i-gat - ed on the E - rie Ca - nal.___

O, Susanna

STEPHEN C. FOSTER

STEPHEN C. FOSTER

Quickly and with humor

1. I____ came from Al - a - ba - ma With my ban - jo on my knee, I'm___
2. I____ had a dream the oth - er night When ev - 'ry-thing was still; I____
3. I____ soon will be in New Or-leans, And then I'll look a - round, And__

goin' to Loui - si - a - na My____ true love for to see; It____
thought I saw Su - san - na A - com - in' down the hill; The__
when I find Su - san - na I'll fall up - on the ground. And__

rained all night the day I left, The weath - er it was dry; The__
buck - wheat cake was in her mouth, The tear was in her eye; Says__
if I do not find____ her, This dark - y'll sure - ly die, And__

sun so hot I froze to death; Su - san - na, don't you cry.
I, I'm com - in' from the south, Su - san - na, don't you cry.
when I'm dead and bur - ied, Su - san - na, don't you cry.

She'll Be Comin' Round the Mountain

Southern Mountain Song
Arranged by Donald Kalbach

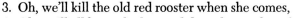

3. Oh, we'll kill the old red rooster when she comes,
4. Oh, we'll all have chicken and dumplings when she comes,
5. Oh, we'll all go out to meet her when she comes,

DANCE

Sets of two couples, facing each other, form a large circle around the room.
(Couple 1 faces counterclockwise. Couple 2 faces clockwise.)

Phrase 1:   Couples, with hands joined, skip forward, bow slightly, and skip
back to place.

Phrase 2:   Couples skip forward and drop hands. Each child links arms with
the child opposite, swings around once, and skips back to place.

Phrase 3:   All four join hands and circle left until each is back in place.

Phrase 4:   Couple 1 skips through the arch made by couple 2. Each couple is
now facing a new couple.

Repeat the whole dance as often as desired.

Music from Making Music Your Own, Book 3   © *Silver Burdett Company 1971*   *Art from* Music for Living, Book 3   © *Silver Burdett Company 1956*

If You're Happy

Traditional
Arranged by James Rooker

Here are other verses to sing:
2. If you're happy and you know it, tap your foot,
3. . . . nod your head,
4. . . . do all three,
Can you add other verses to this happy song?

Jingle Bells

WORDS AND MUSIC BY J. PIERPONT

Dash- ing through the snow in a one - horse o - pen sleigh,

Dash - - ing through the snow in o - pen

O'er the fields we go, laugh - ing all the way;

sleigh. O'er fields we go a - laugh- ing all the

Bells on Bob - tail ring, mak - ing spir - its bright. What

way; The bells are ring - - ing clear and

fun it is to laugh and sing a sleigh - ing song to - night!

bright. What fun to ride to - night!

Music and art from Music in Our Life © *Silver Burdett Company 1959*

Polly Wolly Doodle

TRADITIONAL

AMERICAN FOLK SONG

G

1. Oh, I went down South for to see my Sal, Sing-ing

D7

Pol-ly Wol-ly Doo-dle all the day; My__ Sal, she is a__

G   CHORUS

spunk-y gal, Sing-ing Pol-ly Wol-ly Doo-dle all the day. Fare thee

well, fare thee well, Fare thee well, my fair - y

28

fay, For I'm goin' to Loui-si-an-a, for to

see my Su-sy-an-na, Sing-ing Pol-ly Wol-ly Doo-dle all the day.

2. Oh, my Sal, she is a maiden fair,
   With curly eyes and laughing hair.

3. Oh, a grasshopper sittin' on a railroad track,
   A-pickin' his teeth with a carpet tack.

4. Oh, I went to bed, but it wasn't no use,
   My feet stuck out for the chickens to roost.

5. Behind the barn, down on my knees,
   I thought I heard a chicken sneeze.

6. He sneezed so hard with the whooping cough,
   He sneezed his head and tail right off.

7. The raccoon's tail is very large
   An' the 'possum's tail is bare;
   The rabbit has no tail at all,
   But a little bit a-bunch of hair.

8. The June bug he has golden wings,
   The lightnin' bug has fame;
   The weevil has no wings at all
   But he gets there just the same.

You can add some verses of your own.

Music and art from New Music Horizons, *Fourth Book*   *Copyright by Silver Burdett Company 1945*   **29**

Over the River

WORDS BY LYDIA MARIA CHILDS
OLD SONG

Liltingly

1. O - ver the riv - er and through the wood, To grand- fa - ther's house we
2. O - ver the riv - er and through the wood, Trot fast, ___ my dap - ple

go; _____ The horse knows the way to car - ry the sleigh, Thro'the
gray! _____ Spring o - ver the ground, like a hunt - ing hound, For

white and drift - ed snow. _____ O - ver the riv - er and
this is Thanks - giv - ing Day! _____ O - ver the riv - er and

through the wood, Oh, how the wind does blow! _____ It
through the wood, Now grandmoth - er's face I spy! _____ Hur -

fa mi re do

stings the toes and bites the nose, As o - ver the ground we go.
rah for the fun! Is the pud - ding done? Hur - rah for the pump - kin pie!

Music from Music for Living, Book 2 © *Silver Burdett Company 1956* *Art from* New Music Horizons, First Book *Copyright* **31**
by Silver Burdett Company 1944

Skip to My Lou

AMERICAN PLAY-PARTY SONG

Briskly

1. Flies in the butter-milk, shoo, shoo, shoo! Flies in the butter-milk, shoo, shoo, shoo!
2. Little red wag-on, paint-ed blue, Little red wag-on, paint-ed blue,

mi re do

Flies in the butter-milk, shoo, shoo, shoo! Skip to my Lou, my dar - ling.
Little red wag-on, paint-ed blue, Skip to my Lou, my dar - ling.

3. Lost my partner, what'll I do?
4. I'll find another one prettier than you.
5. Hurry up, slow poke, do, oh, do.

6. One old boat and a run down shoe.
7. Kitten in the hay mow, mew, mew, mew.

Blue-Tail Fly

Southern Folk Song

Arranged by Darrell Peter

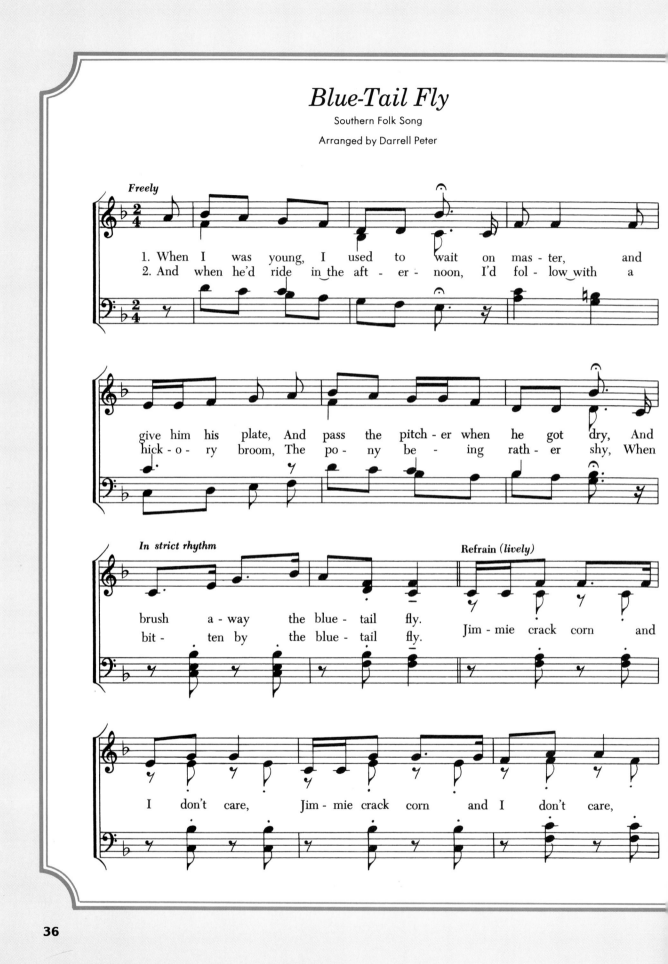

Jim - mie crack corn and I don't care, My mas - ter's gone a - way.

3. One day he rode around the farm;
   The flies so numerous they did swarm;
   One chanced to bite him on the thigh,
   He switched away the blue-tail fly!

4. The pony run, he jump, he pitch,
   He threw my master in the ditch.
   He died, and the jury wondered why—
   The verdict was, "The blue-tail fly!"

5. They laid him under a 'simmon tree;
   His epitaph is there to see;
   "Beneath this stone I'm forced to lie,
   A victim of the blue-tail fly."

Kookaburra

M. Sinclair   Round from Australia

Kook - a - bur - ra sits on an old gum tree, ___

Mer - ry, mer - ry king of the bush is he. ___

Laugh, kook-a- bur- ra, laugh, kook -a- bur- ra, Gay your life must be.

Mister Frog Went A-Courtin'

American Folk Song

Arranged by James Rooker

Brightly

1. Mis-ter Frog went a-court-in' and he did ride, Um-hm! Um-

hm! Mis-ter Frog went a-court-in' and he did ride,

Sword and pis-tol by his side, Um-hm! Um-hm!

2. He said, "Miss Mouse, are you within?"
   "Oh yes, Sir, here I sit and spin."

3. He took Miss Mouse upon his knee,
   And he said, "Miss Mouse, will you marry me?"

4. Oh, where will the wedding supper be?
   Away down yonder in a hollow tree.

Music and art from Making Music Your Own, Book 2 © *Silver Burdett Company 1964* **39**

MARCHING TO PRETORIA

DUTCH FOLK SONG FROM SOUTH AFRICA
ARRANGED BY DARRELL PETER
ENGLISH WORDS BY JOSEF MARAIS

FROM SONGS FROM THE VELD. © 1942. G. SCHIRMER. INC.
USED BY PERMISSION.

Brisk march

VERSE

1. I'm with you and you're with me, And so we are all to-geth-er,
2. We have food, the food is good, And so we will eat to-geth-er,

Simile

So we are all to-geth-er, So we are all to-geth-er.
So we will eat to-geth-er, So we will eat to-geth-er.

Sing with me, I'll sing with you, And so we will sing to-geth-er,
When we eat, 'twill be a treat, And so let us sing to-geth-er,

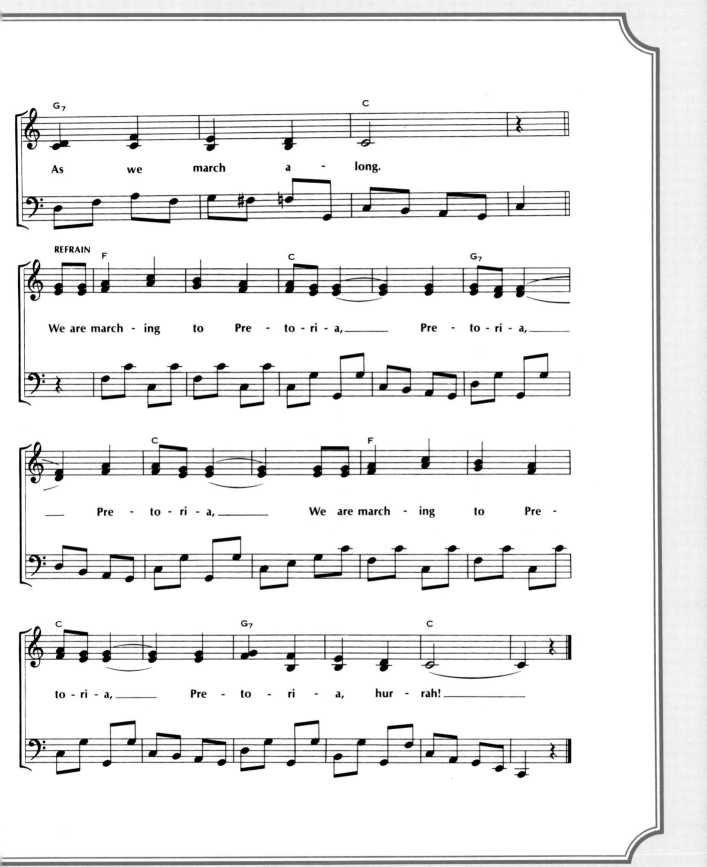

BEST FRIENDS

MUSIC BY CARMINO RAVOSA

ARRANGED BY JAMES ROOKER

WORDS BY MARGARET JONES

Old Dan Tucker   AMERICAN FOLK SONG

ARRANGED BY SCOTT GARRISON

Lively

(A) Old Dan Tuck-er was a might-y man, He washed his face in the fry-ing pan,

Combed his hair with a wag-on wheel, Had a tooth-ache in his heel;

(B) So get out the way, Old Dan Tuck-er; Get out the way, Old Dan Tuck-er;

Get out the way, Old Dan Tuck-er, You're too late to get your sup-per.

Little Ducks

FOLK SONG FROM MARYLAND

Key: F major
Starting note: A (*mi* 3)

Lightly

1. Six lit-tle ducks that I once knew, Fat ones, skin-ny ones,
2. Down to the riv-er they would go, Wibble, wobble, wib-ble, wabble

fair ones too,
to and fro,
} But the one lit-tle duck With a feath-er in his back,

He ruled the oth-ers with a quack, quack, quack, Quack, quack, quack.

He ruled the oth-ers With a quack, quack, quack, quack, quack, quack,

Old MacDonald

TRADITIONAL   ARRANGED BY DONALD SCAFURI

Playfully

Old Mac - Don - ald had a farm, E - I - E - I - O!

1. And on this farm he had some chicks, E - I - E - I - O! With a
2. And on this farm he had some ducks, With a

Chick, chick here, and a chick, chick there,
Quack, quack here, and a quack, quack there,

(L.H.)

Here a chick, there a chick, Ev - 'ry - where a chick, chick.

Here a quack, there a quack, Ev - 'ry - where a quack, quack.

*Repeat these four measures for the additional animal sounds in verses 2-6.

3. Turkeys . . . gobble, gobble
4. Pigs . . . oink, oink
5. Cows . . . moo, moo
6. Horses . . . neigh, neigh

Music from Silver Burdett Music, Kindergarten ⓒ *Silver Burdett Company 1985*   Art from Music *for Living, Book 1* ⓒ *Silver Burdett Company 1956*

I've Been Working on the Railroad

OLD AMERICAN WORK SONG

I've been work-ing on the rail - road, All the live-long day;

I've been work-ing on the rail - road, Just to pass the time a - way.

Don't you hear the whis - tle blow - ing? Rise up so ear - ly in the morn.

Don't you hear the cap - tain shout - ing: ___ "Di - nah, blow your horn!"

Silent Night

Joseph Mohr   Franz Gruber

Arranged by James Rooker

All Night, All Day

NEGRO SPIRITUAL

ARRANGED BY JAMES ROOKER

WHEN THE SAINTS GO MARCHING IN

BLACK SPIRITUAL   ARRANGED BY DONALD KALBACH

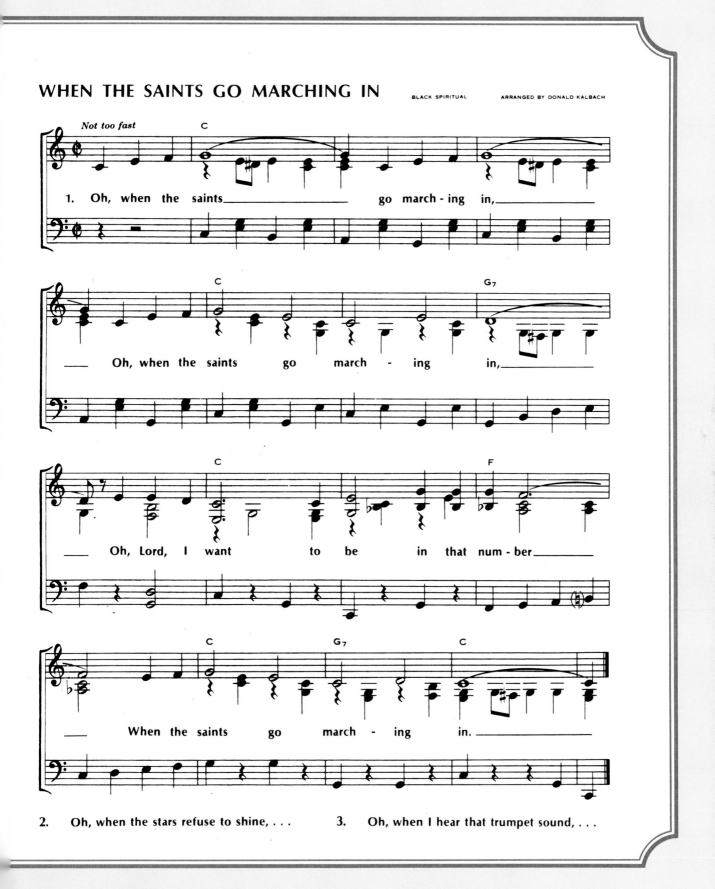

1. Oh, when the saints go march-ing in,

Oh, when the saints go march - ing in,

Oh, Lord, I want to be in that num-ber

When the saints go march - ing in.

2. Oh, when the stars refuse to shine, . . .   3. Oh, when I hear that trumpet sound, . . .

Michael, Row the Boat Ashore

Negro Spiritual

Arranged by Bruce Simpson

Can you add verses of your own? Here are some examples:

1. Noah was a gentle man, Hallelujah!
2. Gabriel, blow the trumpet strong, Hallelujah!
3. Brother, help me turn the wheel, Hallelujah!

Sing your verse as a solo; the class will answer "Hallelujah!"

Eensy Weensy Spider

TRADITIONAL   ARRANGED BY DONALD SCAFURI

The een - sy ween - sy spi - der went up the wa - ter spout;

Down came the rain and washed the spi - der out;

Out came the sun and dried up all the rain; Now the

een - sy ween - sy spi - der went up the spout a - gain.

Mama Paquita

CARNIVAL SONG FROM BRAZIL   ARRANGED BY ROSEMARY JACQUES

ENGLISH WORDS BY MARGARET MARKS

1. Ma - ma Pa - qui - ta,   Ma - ma Pa - qui - ta,
   qui - ta,   Ma - ma Pa - qui - ta,

2. Mama Paquita, Mama Paquita,
Mama Paquita, buy your baby some pajamas,
Some new pajamas, and a sombrero,
A new sombrero that your baby will enjoy,
    ma-ma-ma-ma,

Mama Paquita, Mama Paquita,
Mama Paquita says, "I haven't any money
To buy pajamas and a sombrero,
Let's go to Carnival and dance the
    night away!"

He's Got the Whole World in His Hands

Negro Spiritual

Solo   Chorus

1. He's got the whole _____ world ___ in His __ hands, He's got the
2. He's got the wind and the rain _____ in His __ hands, He's got the

Solo

whole wide _ world ___ in His __ hands, He's got the whole _____ world ___
wind and the rain ___ wind and the rain ___

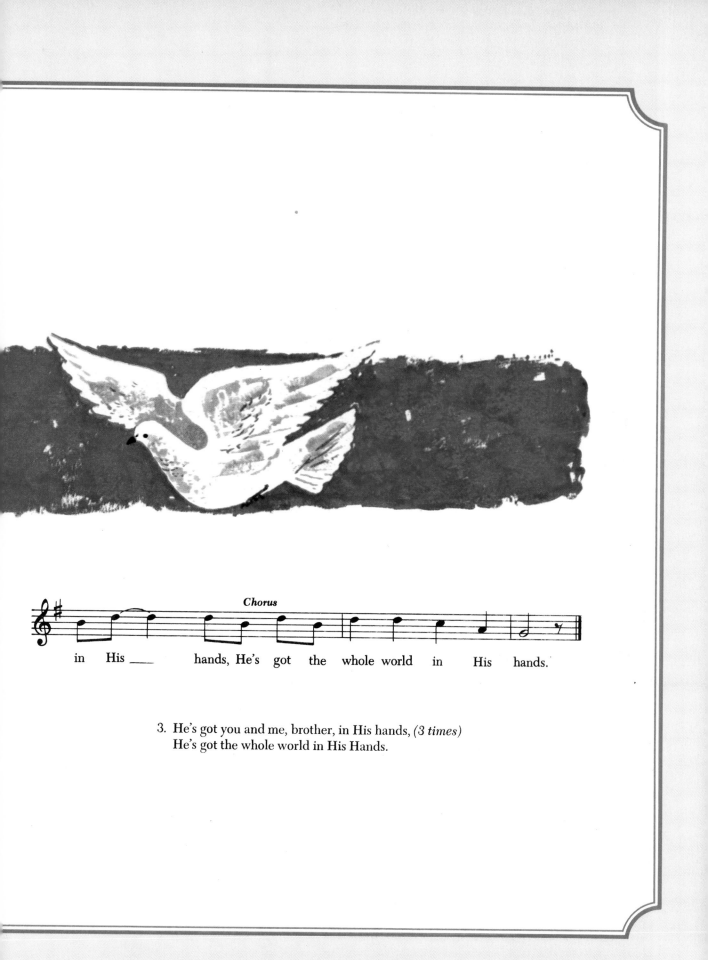

Chorus

in His ___ hands, He's got the whole world in His hands.

3. He's got you and me, brother, in His hands, *(3 times)*
   He's got the whole world in His Hands.

Music from Making Music Your Own, Book 6 © *Silver Burdett Company 1965*   *Art from Music in Our Times* © *Silver Burdett Company 1959*

The Little White Duck

MUSIC BY BERNARD ZARITSKY   ARRANGED BY CAROL KERR

WORDS BY WALT BARROWS

COPYRIGHT 1950, RENEWED 1978 BY GENERAL MUSIC PUBLISHING CO., INC. USED BY PERMISSION.

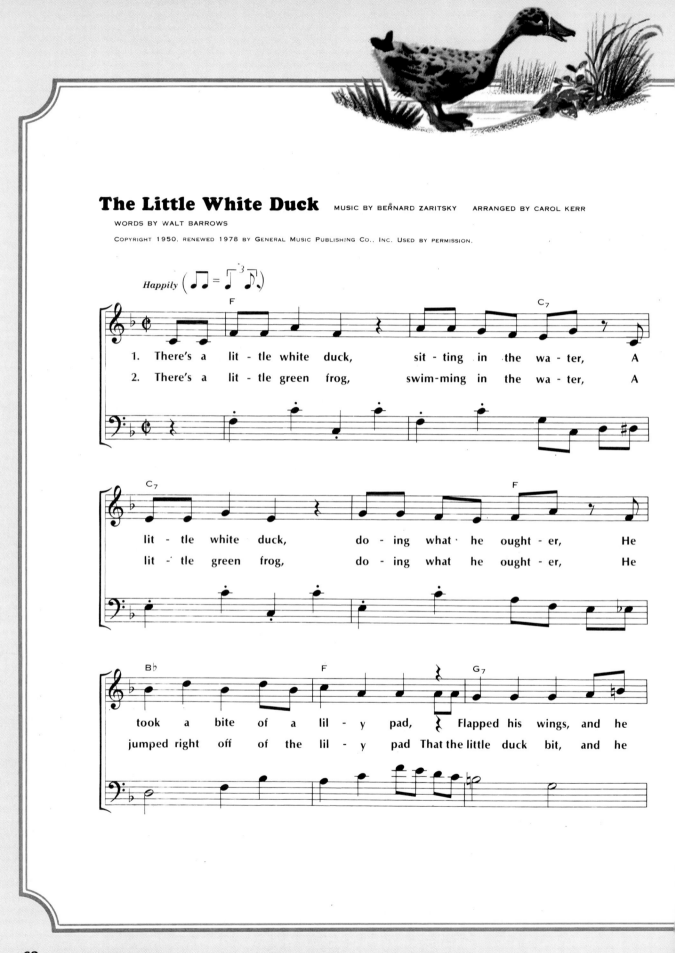

said, "I'm glad I'm a lit-tle white duck, sit-ting in the wa-ter,
said, "I'm glad I'm a lit-tle green frog, swim-ming in the wa-ter,

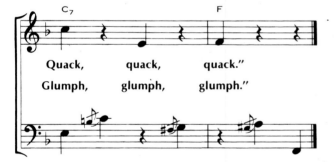

Quack, quack, quack."
Glumph, glumph, glumph."

3. There's a little black bug,
   floating in the water,
   A little black bug,
   doing what he oughter,
   He tickled the frog on the
   lily pad
   That the little duck bit,
   and he said,
   "I'm glad I'm a little black
   bug, floating in the water,
   Chir, chir, chir."

4. There's a little red snake,
   lying in the water,
   A little red snake,
   doing what he oughter,
   He frightened the duck and the
   frog so bad,
   He ate the little bug,
   and he said,
   "I'm glad I'm a little red
   snake, lying in the water,
   Sss, sss, sss."

5. Now there's nobody left,
   sitting in the water,
   Nobody left,
   doing what he oughter,
   There's nothing left but the
   lily pad,
   The duck and the frog
   ran away,
   It's sad that there's nobody
   left, sitting in the water,
   Boo, hoo, hoo.

Hush, Little Baby

Southern Folk Song   Collected by Jean Ritchie
Arranged by Arthur Frackenpohl

2. If that mockingbird won't sing,
   Papa's gonna buy you a di'mond ring.

3. If that di'mond ring turns to brass,
   Papa's gonna buy you a looking glass.

4. If that looking glass gets broke,
   Papa's gonna buy you a billy goat.

5. If that billy goat won't pull,
   Papa's gonna buy you a cart and bull.

6. If that cart and bull turn over,
   Papa's gonna buy you a dog named Rover.

7. If that dog named Rover won't bark,
   Papa's gonna buy you a horse and cart.

8. If that horse and cart fall down,
   You'll be the sweetest little one in town.

Billy Boy

English Folk Song

Can you tell how old Billy Boy's wife is?

1. Oh, __ where have you been, Bil - ly Boy, Bil - ly Boy?
2. Did she bid you to come in, Bil - ly Boy, Bil - ly Boy?

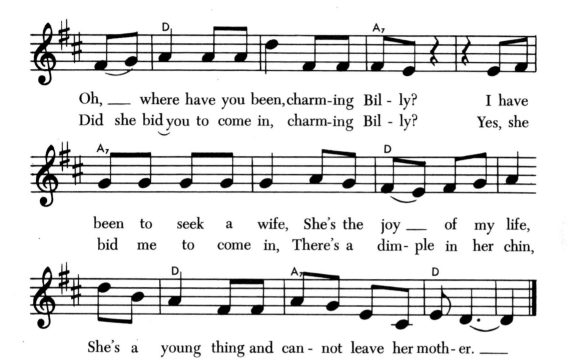

Oh, ___ where have you been, charm-ing Bil - ly? I have
Did she bid you to come in, charm-ing Bil - ly? Yes, she

been to seek a wife, She's the joy ___ of my life,
bid me to come in, There's a dim- ple in her chin,

She's a young thing and can - not leave her moth- er. ___

3. Did she give you a chair, Billy Boy, Billy Boy?
   Yes, she gave me a chair, but there was no bottom there,

4. Can she make a cherry pie, Billy Boy, Billy Boy?
   She can make a cherry pie, quick as a cat can wink her eye,

5. Can she cook and can she spin, Billy Boy, Billy Boy?
   She can cook and she can spin, she can do most anything,

6. How old is she, Billy Boy, Billy Boy?
   Three times six and four times seven, twenty-eight and eleven,

Skin and Bones

Folk Song from Kentucky
Collected by Jean Ritchie

Think of a sound that will make your voice sound spooky.
Listen for the spooky sound in this song.

1. There was an old wom-an all skin and bones, Oo - oo - oo - ooh!

2. She lived down by the old graveyard, Oo-oo-oo-ooh!

3. One night she thought she'd take a walk, Oo-oo-oo-ooh!

4. She walked down by the old graveyard, Oo-oo-oo-ooh!

5. She saw the bones a-layin' around, Oo-oo-oo-ooh!

6. She went to the closet to get a broom, Oo-oo-oo-ooh!

7. She opened the door and BOO!!

Clementine

American Folk Song
Arranged by Bruce Simpson

Floating

1. In a cav-ern by a can-yon, Ex-ca-vat-ing for a mine,

Refrain Oh, my dar-ling, oh, my dar-ling, Oh, my dar-ling Clem-en-tine,

Dwelt a min-er, for-ty-nin-er, And his daugh-ter, Clem-en-tine.

You are lost and gone for-ev-er, Dread-ful sor-ry, Clem-en-tine.

2. Light she was and like a feather,
   And her shoes were number nine;
   Herring boxes without topses,
   Sandals were for Clementine.

3. Drove she ducklings to the water
   Every morning just at nine;
   Struck her foot against a splinter,
   Fell into the foaming brine.

4. Rosy lips above the water
   Blowing bubbles mighty fine;
   But, alas! I was no swimmer,
   So I lost my Clementine.

Dixie

WORDS AND MUSIC BY DAN D. EMMETT

Crisply

1. I __ wish I was __ in the land of cot- ton, Old times there are
   In __ Dix - ie Land __ where __ I was born in, Ear - ly on one
2. There's buck- wheat cakes __ and __ In - dian bat - ter, Makes you fat or a
   Then hoe it down __ and __ scratch your grab- ble, To Dix - ie Land I'm

not for- got -ten, } Look a - way! Look a - way! Look a - way! Dix-ie Land.
frost - y morn- in', }
lit - tle fat - ter, } Look a - way, Look a - way, Look a - way, Dix-ie Land!
bound to trav- el, }

CLAP YOUR HANDS

AMERICAN FOLK SONG   ARRANGED BY ALBERT DeVITO

FROM AMERICAN FOLK SONGS FOR CHILDREN BY RUTH SEEGER.

Clap, clap, clap your hands, Clap your hands to - geth - er,

Clap, clap, clap your hands, Clap your hands to - geth - er.

B Refrain

La la la la la la la, La la la la la la,

La la la la la la la, La la la la la la.

From Making Music Your Own, Book 1 © *Silver Burdett Company 1964*

John Henry

WORK SONG FROM THE DEEP SOUTH

4. Well, the Captain says to John Henry,
   "I believe this mountain's cavin' in."
   John Henry said to the Captain,
   "'Tain't nothin' but my hammer suckin' wind."

5. The man that invented the steam drill
   Thought that he was mighty fine;
   John Henry made his fourteen feet,
   While the steam drill it made only nine.

6. They took John Henry to the buryin' ground,
   And they buried him in the sand;
   And every locomotive come roarin' round
   Says, "There lies a steel-drivin' man."

Do-Re-Mi

WORDS BY OSCAR HAMMERSTEIN II   MUSIC BY RICHARD RODGERS

Let's start at the ver-y be-gin-ning!

Shoo, Fly

American Game Song
Arranged by Cameron McGraw

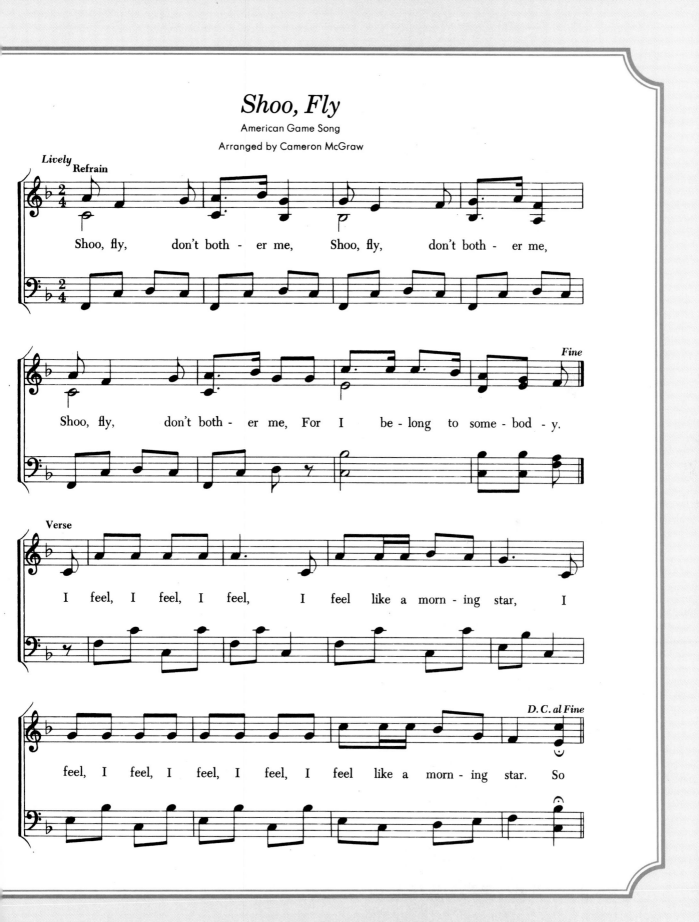

Shoo, fly, don't both - er me, Shoo, fly, don't both - er me,

Shoo, fly, don't both - er me, For I be - long to some - bod - y.

I feel, I feel, I feel, I feel like a morn - ing star, I

feel, I feel, I feel, I feel, I feel like a morn - ing star. So

If I Had a Hammer (The Hammer Song)

Words and Music by Lee Hays
and Pete Seeger
Arranged by Donald Kalbach

f 1. If I had a ham-mer,— I'd ham-mer in the morn-ing,—
p 2. If I had a bell I'd ring it in the morn-ing,—
mf 3. If I had a song I'd sing it in the morn-ing,—
f 4. Well, I got a ham-mer And I got a bell,

SCRATCH, SCRATCH

WORDS AND MUSIC BY HARRY BELAFONTE AND LORD BURGESS

ARRANGED BY LAURA S. WENDEL

Home on the Range

COWBOY SONG

From "Cowboy Songs"
collected by JOHN A. LOMAX

Andante

1. Oh,___ give me a home where the buf - fa - lo roam, Where the deer and the an - te-lope play,___ Where_ nev - er is heard a dis - cour - ag-ing word, And the skies are not cloud - y all day.___

2. Where the air is so pure, and the zeph - yrs so free, The___ breez - es so balm - y and light,___ That I would not ex - change my___ home on the range For___ all of the cit - ies so bright.___

3. How___ of - ten at night when the heav - ens are bright With the light from the glit - ter-ing stars,___ Have I stood there a - mazed and___ asked as I gazed. If their glo - ry ex - ceeds that of ours.___

4. Oh,___ give me a land where the bright dia-mond sand Flows_ lei - sure-ly down___ the stream;___ Where the grace - ful white swan goes_ glid - ing a - long Like a maid in a heav - en - ly dream.___

REFRAIN

Home, home on the range_____ Where the deer and the an-te-lope

play, _____ Where nev-er is heard a dis-cour-ag-ing word, And the

skies are not cloud-y all day._____

Music from The Music Hour, Intermediate Teacher's Book   *Copyright Silver, Burdett and Company 1931*   Art from Music for
Living, Book 4   © *Silver Burdett Company 1956*

Going over the Sea

Collected by Edith Fowke   Canadian Street Rhyme

Arranged by Elizabeth E. Rogers

With a lilt

1. When I was one I ate a bun, Go - ing o - ver the sea. I jumped a - board a sail - or - man's ship, And the sail - or - man said to me,

Refrain

"Go - ing o - ver, go - ing un - der, Stand at at - ten - tion like a sol - dier, With a one, two, and three."

2. When I was two I buckled my shoe,
   Going over the sea.
   I jumped aboard a sailorman's ship,
   And the sailorman said to me,

Canadian Children's Street Rhyme, Adapted   Collected by Edith Fowke   Arranged by Elizabeth E. Rogers   Used by permission

3. When I was three I banged my knee,

4. When I was four I shut the door,

5. When I was five I learned to jive,

6. When I was six I picked up sticks,

7. When I was seven I went to heaven,

8. When I was eight I learned to skate,

9. When I was nine I climbed a vine,

10. When I was ten I caught a hen,

Index